Do Harry agus Stella
Go dtaga bhur ríocht!

Acknowledgements are due to the editors of the following where some of these poems, or versions of them, have been published:

Census 1, 2 and 3 (edited by Sarah Lundberg, Oran Ryan and others), Poems from Phizzfest 2012, Poetry Ireland News, Real Imaginings (edited by Tommy Frank O'Connor), Revival, Riposte, Sunday Miscellany: A Selection from 2008-2011 (edited by Cliodhna Ní Anluain) and Ten Years in the Doghouse (edited by Noel King).

Some have been broadcast on RTE Radio 1 on The Poetry Programme (produced by Aoife Nic Cormaic) and Sunday Miscellany (produced by Cliodhna Ní Anluain).

Scooter won the Francis Ledwidge International Poetry Award 2009.

Sonnet Of a Five-String Banjo was runner-up in the Phizzfest Poetry Competition 2012.

Nine of the poems were written during a residency funded by Dublin City Council at Gaelcholáiste Reachrann in Donaghmede.

The City of Chocolate was commissioned for the Temple Bar Chocolate Festival 2008.

Many thanks to Gilly Cullen for the cover illustration. www.gillycullen.com

Thanks to Noel King, editor, Doghouse Books.

Contents

Three Sextets on Stories

I

Enlightenment

All past reflections shimmer into one:
the apple where Eve's lonely contours shone;
mirrored in their blood, the murdered brides;
in the sea, a horse that one and no one rides;
the gold lid, closed and opened, where Pandora sighs;
and drinking all in, giving all back, Fionn's eyes.

II

Escape

In every human tragedy you feature
among the scathed: the one who gets away,
the torment of the writhing, hollow creature
whose eyes ask only that you see and stay.
All that you've learnt has shrunk, just this you know:
When the enchantment breaks, turn tail and go.

III

Urge

Since there's no cure for curiosity,
you must reach out at last for what must be.
Be it a box, an apple or a land,
it craves the touch of mouth or foot or hand,
craves but the instant where, all past things flown,
the familiar shapeshifts into the unknown.

Strange Familiar

Nor god nor devil brought you.
I neither chose nor own you,
but am bound to you by blood and wonder.

You were the dark shape at my ankles,
weaving between my feet,
one minute clawing the air, all arch and hiss,
the next a soft curl against my breast.

Time was, they might have burnt both of us:
me muttering snatches of rhyme,
you with your constant self-commentary,
your animal companions, your night terrors.

Now you look crooked at me,
your father's fire flickering your nostrils,
and I understand that though he and I
made ourselves whole together,
you made no such contract.

We're caught in that tit for tat:
I too was the spit and image of my father,
a strange familiar to my mother
whose eyes for me were all nonplus and puzzle.

My apron-string kitten,
it seems I turned once in a circle
and found you shapeshifted
to this long-limbed branch-leaper,
walking on air solid as earth,
blending fire and water,
always in your element.

I turn again and catch you
looking out of your Moorish grandmother's
        almond eyes,
eyes cool and clear as heiroglyphs of eyes.

Your skin, opaque as moonlight,
betrays something of your astral travels.

You are making yourself visible
without a spirit guide,
contained enough to conjure
your own familiar.

Contraband

I have smuggled it to England, France, Italy,
    America:
a brown slab wrapped in cling film
taking the space of a holiday read.

And indeed it has its share of stories:
Each time, the baggage x-ray slows, stops.
Its operator studies the dense rectangle,
tries to read it for herself.

It's my mother's brown bread, I say.
If I came without it, I'd be dead.

There is a dusting of flour underneath
so it won't stick to the roasting tins,
and only the roasting tins are big enough.

The crust is the colour of fudge,
the inside a shade paler.
It looks solid but has a soft bounce of air.
It conjures up my mother's fingers
barely touching the sticky dough,
in her head that elusive recipe.
Whenever we asked,
she said, *this one was only thrown together*.
Something was missing or forgotten,
there'd been no buttermilk, or oatmeal.
When she made it properly, she'd let us know.

The pony-tailed security guard
calls her colleague over.
Once he's sure it is, in fact, bread,
he sighs and asks if I am carrying
any other drugs or weapons.

I do not carry drugs or weapons,
but my knife was always ready
when the bread was slid from the oven.
In vain my mother wrapped the steaming loaf
in a checked tea-towel
to try to fend us off.

You'll garter it, she told us.
It won't cut till it cools down.
But we each hacked a ragged slice,
slathered it in cold butter.

It'll stick in your craw when it's too hot, she'd say.
We'd giggle, ask her where our craws were,
and ignore the ache between our lungs
where the warm dough lodged.

I do not carry drugs or weapons
but the bread contains a mind-altering substance,
distorts your perception of time and place,
brings you back ten, fifteen, twenty years
to the kitchen table, the smell of home.

I do not carry drugs or weapons
but my mother supplies this for free
even after you are hooked,
and on every journey you're a courier.

In England, France, Italy, America,
when I share my mother's brown bread,
it's familiar as an old book,
and old friends ask if I have the recipe yet.

I don't think I'll ever manage it.
There's some knack to the way
the table under our elbows becomes home
and the years dissolve in our mouths.

Three Poems for my Father

I
Cut Off

My father worked with the Electricity Board.
He was a power surge that turned night to day,
made the streetlamps dawn pink one by one
and the yellow light leap down the street.

My father was plugged in to everything.
He was gadget man
with his electric potato-peeling bowl,
his syphons, flares and phase testers,
his occasional swims against the current.

He said, *let there be light*,
but sometimes hid his under a bushel:
At night the faintest glow kept him awake.
He made a lid to cover the digital radio clock.
Even the TV's standby light, he taped over.

He had delicate hands for the works of old clocks,
but on holidays complained
of a grandfather chime in the hall
or a church bell that mourned the quarter hour:
He hated to hear time measured out.

On the night of his wake, we were suddenly cut off.
Floods separated the suburbs,
the kettle stayed stone-cold.
His gerry-rigged system went haywire
and light buckled across the world.

II
Always Not There

You are always
not there, now.
When I wonder
about your father's house in Turnabarsun,
or who fathered a second cousin's child;
when three teenagers banjax
the sofa bed during the World Cup;
when a door scrapes the floor and needs shortening;
when it's a question of the best way to do something,
to get somewhere,
you are always not there.

You were a problem solver.
There was nothing you liked better
than to look over your glasses at a broken thing,
till it provoked you into
reaching out the perfect tool
from your endless store of
pliers, tweezers, staple guns, wire cutters.

You could draw a plan of
the *cúl tí* bed set into the hearth,
write an encyclopaedia of family secrets,
draw a freehand map of Ireland,
get from here to Ringsend
without passing a traffic light.

And we don't mind splitting the bill,
but we miss your sly pleasure in paying:
You were always at the table's head,
discreetly gesturing to the waiter,
keeping everyone's hands in their pockets,
at your happiest the day I told you
you were a great provider.

And what our eyes say when we meet
over celebrations and casual dinners,
is that the table looks off-kilter since
you are always not there.

III
The God of Unravelling

My dad was the god of unravelling.
He unpicked the cord on brown paper parcels
while we begged to rip them open.
That's a grand piece of string, he'd say.

Flexes and wires he knew
like the knotted veins in his hands,
where each began, ended and intertwined
behind his big chair in the corner.

He was a dab hand at taking knots
out of gold and silver chains,
methodically smoothing the ganglions into strands,
which he laid side by side on our polished table.

When we showed off our muscles,
flexing the small bumps on our arms,
he would assess them, and say with his slow smile,
I've seen bigger knots in thread.

My mother's bag of wool,
a spaghetti mess of blues and reds,
he would subdue into neatly rolled balls,
his thickened fingers worrying the nests apart.

He had no time for yoga or meditation,
but his busy brain lost itself
in the cool analysis of chaos,
the challenge of a tangle.

No Word for Him

The man on the radio
who has lost his child
says there is
no word for him.

If I lost my wife, I'd be a widower, he says.
If I lost my parents, I'd be an orphan,
but there is no word for you
when you lose a child.

The man on the radio
speaks a grief so unnatural
that no noun or verb
can express it.

The dictionary is bereft
for the man on the radio.
He is a bone in the throat of language,
a word lost for words.

Grandmother Daedalus

Sunlight was the enemy of my maternal grandmother.

Earthed in the half-light of her kitchen,
she shunned the excess of the sky.
The shades were drawn in her parlour
so midday could not wilt the chintz roses
or spotlight the dust motes that soared accusingly.

Daily she scrubbed ceiling to cellar:
She could not fathom
how her rooms harboured floaters and feathers,
suspected that the sun created dust.

Sunlight was the enemy of my maternal grandmother.

She kept her pantry dark and cool
for the sun spoiled butter, milk, meat.
There was no end to the folly
of those who courted it.

On hot days she drank scalding tea in the shade,
wore a battered hat as she beat dust out of carpets
and kept her face and arms covered,
for only labourers and washerwomen got a tan.
Even her front door wore a blind
to stop its paint blistering.

Sunlight was the enemy of my maternal grandmother.

She shook her head when jetlines
    scored the summer sky.
When God wants me up there, He'll call me, she'd say.
He called her too early, and my child mind
could not imagine her solid form
floating to any heaven.

Now when I see the property supplements
I think of her:
Soak up the sun in this light-flooded jewel.
Head above the clouds in this pied-à-terre.

I imagine her reading them
in the time she never had,
twitching like a Roman blind with exasperation
and warning, *we'll all melt in this heat.*

In Defence of Chocolate

Eating chocolate is not a sin,
and cakes cannot be wicked,
whatever the magazines say.

Au contraire, oh *éclair*:
Eating chocolate is a religious experience,
unless you covet your neighbour's chocolate
or kill him for it.

Keeping chocolate is the opposite of a sin.
You can use it to honour your father and mother,
share it with your neighbour and his wife.

Making chocolate mousse is a corporal good work
that feeds the hungry,
a spiritual good work
that comforts the sorrowful.
You take three eggs
and 200 grammes of dark chocolate.
You need only 170 grammes
but the other thirty keep the cook virtuous.
Separate the eggs, and whip the whites
till they are bright and stiff as archangels' wings,
or billow white as summer clouds,
cumulo nimbus, floating close to heaven,
the kind that cherubs sit upon.

Melt the chocolate in a *bain-marie*.
I like to think it's named for the Virgin Mary,
because anyone blessed
with an immaculate conception
can surely bathe without touching the water.

Beat your trinity of yolks into the chocolate,
and stir a little spirit in:
brandy, cointreau, if you must, *Lacryma Christi*.
Then, fold in the egg whites
till you have God's good air
trapped in a layer of chocolate.

As long as you're not too proud of it,
your chocolate mousse
will smooth your path to heaven,
helping you to love your enemies,
and your neighbour as yourself.

The City of Chocolate

Chocolate is a fairytale
with ugly sisters feasting at the ball
and Cinderella working in the ash;

with the giant thundering above the stalk
and Jack and his mother going
from subsistence to starvation.

Chocolate is an exotic empire,
a city of dark squares and bitter streets,
an ancient democracy destroyed.

Mayans, rich and poor, drank the dark froth
till Aztecs turned their beans to currency,
their farmers to slaves,
their foam to an elixir.

We pluck it from a shelf,
unwrap the glossy paper, glitzy foil,
place a tablet to melt on our tongues
or snap it quickly and secretly.

They pluck the ripe pods, large as melons,
split and scrape,
spread seeds and pulp to dry in the sun,
then pack the yield, too precious to be tasted.

Chocolate is an ambiguous relationship,
the too-sweet encounter, the sharp aftertaste,
too much or too little
of a good thing.

Alone with its dark savour,
your mouth hears its own sound,
a soft hum that resonates
in your head and throat.

Chocolate is lexicon of exotic words:
Olmec, Izapan, Mayan, Aztec,
Tabasco, Yucatan, Guatemala,
a sound that began with X or K,
a kiss that we couldn't pronounce, a betrayal,
always harvested by the poor of one place
for the wealthy in another:

Remember as your hand
brings that exquisite square to your mouth
that some who live hand to mouth
built this delicious city.

And yes, there are princes
who fight dragons to set workers free,
and sisters who share the spoils
and giants who tumble down.

This is how the city's contours soften,
how its heart expands and melts
till Jack's mythic, magic beans are worth a cow
and he can enter the City of Chocolate now.

White, Too

AJ: *I thought black was death?*
Meadow: *White too.*
- *The Sopranos*, discussing Frost's *Stopping by Woods on a Snowy Evening*

White, too? There's not a colour can escape.
Death's palette will all other boards eclipse.
Your memory takes on every shade and shape.

The silks that now over your casket drape,
like those you loved beneath your fingertips:
white, too. There's not a colour can escape.

The freesia petals, hollow as the nape
of eager neck that calls out to my lips:
Your memory takes on every shade and shape.

The chalice filled with some beloved grape:
Rhone red, that rosé you eked out in sips,
white, too. There's not a colour can escape.

The crematorium's grey curtains gape
and billow to the contour of your hips:
Your memory takes on every shade and shape.

The night you crumpled up your dress of crêpe
and melted, melting me. . . .The candle drips
white, too. There's not a colour can escape:
Your memory takes on every shade and shape.

Black Stuff

I grew up near the Guinness houses:
Corrib Road, where no river flowed
but the black stuff, delivered in crates at Christmas
to ould lads proud of the grand job.
Guinness was good for them:
Arthur gave them their pension,
fed their crate-load of children
from pint-sized to full of bottle,
gave girls and boys alike their first moustache,
rented them houses till they could buy them out.

I like its colour, muddy as the Liffey;
the way its black and beige dust motes
separate, settle into coffee and cream
in the time it takes to tell a story,
catch your breath;
its taste of roast and toast, that first sweet sup,
warm from the tap. You can't sup beer or lager,
that lightness on your lip
could never be more than a sip.
And porter carries many a conversation still:
No beer is so hotly debated, so coldly assessed.
The perfect temperature's a keg's worth of chat,
even the distance to the barrel
is worth mulling over.

Last year we found a short tap in Tralee,
settled like slow pints at a corner table,
and parted with the landlady like family.

What better drink for your last request?
No claret inking thin glass,
or brandy burning in a great balloon
could see you off like the contemplation
of those last slow breaths rising and falling
till the head stands proud of the body.

Stowaways

The woman around the corner
says country people are taking over Dublin.

She says you can see the return tickets
floating down the Liffey every Monday morning.
Country people are letting on
they're coming up for the weekend,
then the cute hoors are stowing away,
getting jobs in the newspapers,
running the civil service,
writing speeches for TDs
and signing grants for the relations.

I think of them crouched in the leaky hold of the city,
sharing a damp cabin with hard-up Dubliners.
or washed up in that bedsit that made me cry:
the room split in three with hardboard partitions,
like a home-made doll's house,
the one window favouring the living room,
the kitchen and bedroom lightless,
the old landlord inviting me to sit
in a chair pushed against one wall,
my feet touching the blinded fireplace on the other
and tears itching my eyes.

For years I hoped whoever lived there
had some happiness to fall back on
and got out alive.

The woman around the corner
wouldn't trust anyone from outside Dublin.

Just because they're from two counties away
doesn't mean they're not immigrants, she says.
To be honest, she's not sure
about people from the northside either,
but as long as they cross the river again after work,
she says she's happy enough,
though she never looks it.

We Buy Gold

We buy your memories and heirlooms by weight.
They are worth less than you think,
the family's gilded candlesticks,
or your great grandmother's rose gold wedding band,
engraved with her name and his.

In the photograph over the piano,
she displays it shyly
against the home-made Charleston dress,
run up in secret after she took the original
home from the draper's on 'appro'.

Her ring feels heavy on your hand,
but the long years you kept it safe
and got by without pawning it
weigh nothing to us.

Your mementoes are scrap metal.
We erase their individuality:
The names on the ring, the roses on the earrings.
We ungild your lilies and discard the flowers.

Those treasures that a line of daughters
massaged with soft cloths,
swaddled and tucked into boxes,
we merge with the heirlooms of others.

We subtract the weight
of stones you think are precious.
You do not have to remove them,
but we cannot take them into account.

Gravity exerts little claim
on your gold-plated crucifix.
We weigh sentimental value
and find it wanting.

We do what it says on the sign:
We buy yellow gold, white gold, rose gold,
wedding bands, engagements rings,
chains, pendants, earrings,
bracelets, bangles, damaged pieces, dental gold,
coins, nuggets & bullion.

We won't encourage you
to prise the fillings from your teeth,
but if they happen to fall out,
we will certainly give you a price.

Time was, our business seemed shameful,
lurking down darker lanes,
but the age of recycling
has made us respectable.
We are brightly lit, we choose main streets,
we are all business.

We are reverse alchemists:
We may not turn your gold to tin,
but we show that your emperor
had you fooled all along.

We melt memories down
to their essential elements.
We don't deal in dreams or histories,
we buy gold.

Grange Abbey, Donaghmede

It's a shell marooned on a suburban shore,
a shell that we scarcely listen to:
Open your ears!

Under the tide of traffic there's a faint rush of sea;
the wind singing in the golden meadows;
the shouts of men hoisting keystones;
the stone-cutter at the grave slabs.

Here lies a way of life:
the church itself a gravestone now,
the graveyard a park, unloved as parks go,
a local traversy, a travesty
of stripped bicycles and shopping trolleys.

Here lies the Grange of Baldoyle:
a medieval supermarket, a busy farm
with daily deliveries on carts or foot
into the spreading town.

Open your ears!
Can you hear the King of Leinster's coach,
hear his great lungs breathe in the country air?
That's the scratch of his quill
gifting his gleaming fields to city monks.

Open your ears!
Hear the din of dinner at the Priory of All Hallows:
Trinity monks sup milk from Baldoyle cows,
feed on Grange cheeses, bread and butter,
quaff St Donagh's mead.

And we should drink deep from this well of history:
These walls guard secrets still,
have barely teased the archeologists
with splinters of bowls and bones,
a riddle of shifted stones.

Open your ears!
A whole world quivers like a slammed door
in this shell washed up on a suburban shore.

Badger

I've never seen you alive:
You're from stories, riverbank tales
of a gentleman in a dinner jacket,
the solid citizen who prevails.

A mystery like your name:
Are you badged head or corn-hoarder,
or grey man, the Irish *broc*,
a fugitive living on the border?

Holing up in a dug-out,
solitary or thick as thieves,
covering miles in the night
to reach a safe house, eaves-
dropping on your foes without a sound,
giving no quarter when you clamp down.

Giant Panda

There was excess postage on the package
for the *Musée d'Histoire Naturelle*
Père David sent back from China
in 1896. Out of it fell

a monochrome pelt,
a skeleton and a few lines about amazing weeks
in the Himalayas, finding a raccoon-faced lumberer
in woods amid jagged peaks.

The bear with its dark spectacles in a white face,
the priest with his cassock, white collar and
        air of distinction,
both camouflaged in the dapple sun on snow,
all light and shadow, loners on the brink of extinction.

A carnivore turned vegetarian, barely surviving
on its own bodyweight of bamboo,
a missionary no longer converting the native gods
into something palatable. Poor you:

Stuck between opium wars and bouts over tea,
your specimens damaged by assistants
        who didn't care,
the music you hated, the burden of trunks and cases,
your golden monkey skins perishing in the humid air.

Before you return to Tientsin, where the Christians
        are dead,
ten Daughters of Charity murdered, your mission
        house blazing,
if only everything could stop at this moment
        that knows
nothing but the quiet eyes of a new bear, gazing.

Queen of the May

I won't wash my face in the dew at first light:
I never had that maiden skin, rose pink or
    hawthorn white.
Mine is oil and olive, the dawn water
would run off me like a mother's warning.

I won't heed my grandmother's *piseogs*,
the way she kept the may out of the house
and crossed herself if we came through the door
clutching its starry branches.

No, I'll cross the threshold of summer
    with a bold stride,
bringing in stars like a promise of harvest.
I'll close my eyes to the shadow of the scythe,
toss my hips at virgins and fairies,
and defy them to deny me
my blooming crown, my sweet bouquet,
    my *objets trouvés* of summer.

I'll heap clusters of flowers on my altar
and be my own Queen of the May,
and I won't believe in anything
except that summer is coming
and May needs nothing else to be magic.

I'll drink wine in the long twilight
with my love in the garden,
lie in the grass and love freckles onto his skin.
I'll dance at his maypole with nothing to lose
but my chains of daisies that each say, *he loves me*.

Oh you might as well talk to the wall
(that's crawling with woodbine again)
as lay down the law to me,
feckless and reckless with summer.

Poem for October

October is a greedy month:
Night gobbles at the edges of day;
the forest floor breaks the leaves down
to a dull mulch in the earth's mouth;
the woods hide misers' hordes
and spectres door to door
cross into the other world
as if there were no tomorrow.

October is a prickly time
of beech burs and chestnut spines,
of sweaters that scratch and scarves that itch
your faded summer skin.
Every autumn, I want to burrow down,
muffle up against the chill,
swaddle and hide in a thicker skin
till spring lets the sunshine in.

But today I saw chestnuts fall in the park.
My daughter said they were prickly apples,
whispering jokes and bursting with laughter,
the mahogany shining through their slit skirts.
Ah, the chestnuts know how to come out in winter:
They cast themselves into the unknown,
leaping from trees onto crispy leaves,
shedding their thick green dresses.

While humans huddle, the chestnut is saying,
look at me, polished for the autumn!
Tie me to a string and I'll swing all around me.
I am not afraid of any season: I contain a whole world.

Next autumn I'll be a green leaper,
throwing off my thick skin and fighting my corner,
shining a brown light into the winter,
knowing I'm big as a tree inside.

Reines Claudes Dorées

We came to Beaugas in the heatwave
to harvest your greengages
and found the *Reine Claudes Dorées*,
a queen's ransom in the trees.

I felt myself full of promise,
a life three weeks inside me,
so new I told you only
to turn away your *eau de vie*.

On the orchard grass, bittersweet windfalls
blown down before their time.
It had happened twice before,
but this time I felt fruitful, sure.

Between mornings and afternoons of picking
      golden fruit,
leaping for high branches,
stripping them almost bare,
we rested in the shade at noon.

I sat warm on a fallen tree
with my love, my friend, my friend's love, and
      my child-to-be,
with plums like sunshine bursting in my mouth
and thought, *this is enough*.

Sometimes the fruit was sticky:
Insects had got there first,
their entrance marked by
a thin trickle of honey.

And, though overnight we kept the plums
cool as the baking dark allowed,
their bloom had lost a shade by morning
for their trip to *la coopérative*.

Queen Claude would be forgotten
except for these small fruits:
Her years a bare two dozen,
her back bent almost double,
her memory is made perfect by
these gold globes streaked with green,
misty like opals,
luscious.

In the gloom of our summer,
I think of your orchard
where for a week we panned for gold
in rivers of *Reine Claude* trees.

With nuggets big as walnuts
we packed the wooden boxes,
our arms and mouths and bellies
so full,
      so full,
           so full.

Transformer

You crashland on the planet,
sleeping till a quake rips a ravine
across the world, the old wounds erupting,
unearthing the ghost in the machine.

A robot shifting to a rocket ship,
simple enough to blast imagination.
Small fingers, minds earth their magic in you,
hypnotising themselves into a fascination.

Shrinking into yourself, or big enough
to save or scoff the race,
you're more than meets the eye,
a bridge from outer to inner space.

You relish your own language:
Autobot, Decepticon, Vector Sigma,
the earth's fate lisping in your mouth,
little shapeshifter, changeling, enigma.

Scooter

Between our sure steps you pick your way
slowly at first, one foot ticking on the path,
the other planted on your new scooter.

Quickly, unexpectedly,
you stutter into your stride
till you are gliding, feet together,
just ahead.

While we exchange shy smiles of pride
you are suddenly farther on,
heartshockingly small beside the open road,
a skater on cracked ice
where big children knife by on bicycles.

There's a flashback to that first crawl
when the house bulged with dangers:
The fireplace a bludgeon for your head,
the table corner a spike for your eye,
the kitchen a nerve centre of poisons and avalanches.

Now we gasp into a run
at your heedless happiness
as you round the corner,
as we round the corner,
watching the gap widening.

Night Before School

It had rained all day, driving round Inverin
    and Moycullen,
the landscape smudged like a child's painting,
the road a wet blackboard.

You slept most of the way home to Dublin,
your longest nap since you curled in a sling
just the other side of my womb.

I was the one stir crazy,
knowing what was ahead of you:
hemmed into a uniform, a small desk and chair,
the compulsory sitting, your ceaseless chatter stifled.

And then the sun blessed us with a last kick
    of summer,
our small garden golden and glittering with drops,
the apples glowing fairytale red.

We postponed dinner for Poddle Park.
You pedaled an heirloom bike through
    the slanting light
and I walked behind, drinking you in,
seeing how summer had grown you.

In my shadow I'm a big girl, you laughed,
and the late sun flung a long figure on a high nelly
stretching away from us
over the shaking grass.

Two Slices of Ham

My grandmother was a great woman for hospitality.
You'll have a diamond of apple tart, she'd say,
a cup of tea in your hand,
another cut of bread and a slice of ham.

Often when she'd persuaded
the visitor in the living room to accept
something she didn't have in the kitchen,
she'd rap on the window,
calling me from garden to back door.

Run down to Mattses and get us two slices of ham,
    she'd whisper.
Go out the side way now –
and if you fall, don't wait to get up.

I puzzled over her words
as I raced down the narrow passage,
snagging my jumper on the hedge.

The bladed wheel on the meat-slicer slid slowly
and the shopman crooned, *All I have to do*
    is dre-e-e-eam.
I hopped from foot to giddy foot,
nervous that my Gran would be caught out.

When I got back she'd be waiting at the back door,
the bread buttered, ready to slip the ham between.
The blessings of God on you, she'd say.

She'd appear calmly in the living room,
place a full plate in her visitor's hand,
and smiling, enjoy their enjoyment
of all she had, and more.

Four Poems for Harry

I
A Word for Love

I want to roll you around on my tongue
like a fabulous word,
something with a hint of Italian swagger
for your Neapolitan blood:
Carravaggio, bragadoccio, imbroglio;
something muscular and supple,
hard with a soft centre or vice versa:
lascivious, basilica, scintillating;
a phrase to make me drunk and sluttish:
my *uisce beatha*, my lilac wine, my *coteaux de layon*,
then tremble on the edge of sobriety:
my honeysuckle, my hot posset, my dark chocolate.
I want to roll you around on my tongue
like a phonetic alphabet:
my bilabial fricative, my uvular lateral, my plosive,
my glottal
stop.

II
Wine Growers

I want to love you like old growers love their vines
on the unkinder slopes of western France:
On winter nights they sleep out in their groves,
better to feel the treacherous frost advance,
then dip the buds in water, shoot by shoot,
to freeze a halo round each growing fruit.

If not with water, then with fire they love:
haul braziers out to keep their darlings warm,
and even fire down rockets on their crops
when jaundiced skies portend a summer storm.

I want to love if not with water then with fire;
making a halo for my throat's desire,
sky-rocketing to save you from the storm,
sleeping out among your roots to keep you warm.

III
Wedding Sonnet

We come together here to speak the vow
our eyes first made, above the lily-pond
where two reflections shimmered into one,
outside the sunny Silk Road restaurant.

The road beneath our feet is grass and stone.
Its length of seven years behind us charts
our silk route, ribboning from Kimmage West,
its trade, the secrets of our minds and hearts.

And though we don't know where this road
        may weave,
over what fells and edges it might travel,
we know our home is in each other's arms,
our two yarns spun together can't unravel.

Two perfect equals, plying a fair trade,
exchange today the vows our eyes once made.

IV
Waking at Tara Cove

Light trembles on lashes. Your eyes
stir deep pools of morning
where I might float or drown.
Your body dawns on me,
our mouths dock and anchor
where the earth ends and the sea begins,
where the sea ends and the earth begins.
We reclaim each other,
snatching a space from the time that rushes in,
as though this moment of skin on flesh on skin

could absolve the blanked out, the blackouts,
the sodden sheets, the drunken bouts,
the one-night stands, the one-stand nights,
the cracks in your heart, the rips in my tights.

Holding you now against all we've weighed
        and wanted
and feeling love tilt the balance on our side:
We're still looking into each other's surprised eyes
and casting off, with a blessing instead of a curse,
the ones that should have been better,
the ones that could have been worse.

Rosemary

The first time we stood in my garden
you admired the rosemary:
holding its hundred arms aloft,
rubbing shoulders with us,
making a charmed circle.

You closed your eyes,
bruised a stem in your hands, took a long breath,
and in the heart of summer I inhaled winter, incense,
all my Christmases.

Where rosemary flourishes, you said, *the woman rules
    the house,*
and somehow it thrives here under my neglect.
I am grateful for its permanence, glad of its power,
and though I need no ointment, salve or liniment,
I have only to reach my arm to find
a sprig for my pillow to ward off witches,
a tea for headaches, wine for gout, a purseful
    against plague,
an oil to mummify, a torch to purify,
a spear for friendship, remembrance, love.

My grandmother said rosemary never grew taller
    than Christ
nor older than his years on earth.
We have two decades yet before we know for sure.

Meanwhile ours is rich and handsome
and we are rosemary spendthrifts,
turning shoulders and legs of lamb into porcupines
with forests of fragrant spines,
studding the roast pork,
sprinkling the salads,
spiking the summer potatoes,
stirring it through Italian sauces.

In summer, when our daughter is asleep,
the garden calls us out.
We drink in the last of the light
and breathe the incense inching up the wall.
Brighter greens come and go, but always
it is dark green above, downy grey under,
and suddenly a scatter of lilac stars.

Something Out of Nothing Soup

When you call from France
I say I'm writing about food
and you remind me of the soup I made
in our London bedsit.

While one of us cooked,
the other soaked in the big bath in the kitchen
figuring out new ways to fool
the metre that gobbled our fifty pences.

Working yet another 'back week' in the '80s,
cash poor, dream rich,
we'd shop in Sainsbury's
heaping our trolley with luxuries.

Your favourite was a steeply-priced cheesecake,
the glossy fruit encased in ruby jelly,
the cream cheese impossibly high and white,
the base pale as champagne.

Our mouths watered as you placed it
high at the front of the trolley
where other people put small children.

As we nosed towards the checkout
we took everything out again:
chocolate biscuits, ginger crackers, your father's
    gourmet relishes,
we replaced on reproachful shelves.

Last of all,
you'd bring the cheesecake carefully back to its fridge
as I crossed the last aisle.
Some day, you'd say.

At the checkout we'd pay for
our bag of flour, our bread and porridge.
We lived on pancakes for a fortnight.
When the eggs ran out, and then the milk,
we made them from flour and water.

And one evening for a change,
I decided to make soup.
There was nothing to make soup with
but I boiled water anyway,
made a stock of salt and pepper
and dried herbs left by a previous tenant.

It was delicious, savoury,
we relished its simplicity.
you said God was not the only one
who could make something out of nothing.

When at last I got paid, I bought the cheesecake
        for you.
I carried it to the counter like an offertory gift.
It was the day you turned the telly on its side
so you could watch it lying on the sofa.

Side-by-side we bit into
the taste of disappointment:
The cream cheese stuck to the roofs of our mouths,
its fruit artificially sweet, its base soft and sickly.

I'd thought we would treasure the time
we finally ate that cheesecake,
but on the phone from France
your voice is warm with the memory of
Something out of Nothing Soup.

Herb Garden

What I wanted was a little order:
A grid of beds where monks might meditate
saying their office from border to border,
herbs for cures and cooking, aromatics for incense,
a medieval makeover for the garden.

What we have is a lava of mismatched pots:
The bronze feathers of fennel, mint rampant,
    lavender ragged,
lemon balm half-blacked by frost,
two kinds of parsley, flat-leaved and curly,
a waterfall of chives,
the thriving coriander stripped one night
    of all its leaves,
the thyme that has died twice,
the rosemary tree, a stout washerwoman
    in blue-flowered sleeves,
growing new arms by the day.

All summer we plundered them for salads,
thrilled by our fledgling domesticity.
Now, though winter has whitened the lavender,
and parsleys, chives and fennel hold their breaths,
the mint is still stubbornly green.

I pluck armfuls of rosemary for roasts and wreaths,
and the cracked stems exhale fir-trees and chest-rubs.
I am dizzy with a scent that says only the year
    is dying,
that some of us come through unscathed,
that we are either immortal
or there is no cure for us.

Jazzy Surrey Sunday

It's Sunday and the Miles Davis Quintet
is juggling *The Surrey with the Fringe on Top*.
John Coltrane is flinging the notes into the air.
When he takes us out in the surrey,
when he takes us out in the *Sir! Sir! Sir!*
the surreal gig that takes to the sky
as though reindeer or unicorns
were making it fly.

When he takes us out in
the saxophone with the fringe on top,
the saxophone with the dinge on top,
the lunatic fringe of the melody
going on a binge of improv.

It's a jigsaw of a rickshaw,
whose pieces float in space,
weightlessly whirr near the original shape
of the shiny little surrey,
the blurry little surrey,
then blast into smithereens.

When he flakes us out in the surrey,
when he breaks right out of the surrey,
the wheels are yellow,
the feel is mellow,
the dashboard's genuine hell for leather,
we've an elephant's eye on the heavenly weather.
It's oh what a bountiful morning
in the surrogate surrey with the fringe on the top.

Sonnet of a Five-String Banjo

An African mother in the Appallachians
gave birth to my flat-bellied incantations.
I'm fingerpickin', real hot lickin',
giddy to the neck like a headless chicken.
I'm a sleight of hand, a one-man band,
a corny, born-again journeyman.
I'm a god, a gourd, a hurdy-gurdy,
I'm a country girl that's plain and purdy.
I'm a country boy, Mama's pride and joy,
I'm all wound up like a clockwork toy.
I'm a *pequeniño*, a pickaninny,
a shindig granny, a hootenanny.
I'm a coal miner, a gold miner,
a moonshiner, a lonesome piner.
In a grass of my own, I'm blue and new,
I'm rare old, fair old mountain dew.

I'm a railroad car sliding down the fret,
I'm a runaway freight but I'll run back yet.
I'm a lonesome whistle, hopin' this'll
pierce your heart like a fresh-picked thistle.
I'm a square dancer, a quare dancer,
a bit of a chancer with a smart answer.
I'm a necromancer, a patched pantser,
an old time, gold time rhyme romancer:
I'm a banjo, I'm a banshee,
you can ban everybody but you can't ban me.
(No sirree)
I'm flailin' and wailin' like an old banshee,
You can ban anybody but you
can't
ban
me
(dum-diddley-i-die)
not me!

Johnny Cash Sings *Hurt*

You creak out this last confession
walking a sound between prayer and sob,
eyes looking death in the face,
heart on its last throb.

You've always known these bars
you're breaking through, these blues,
the man in black depression,
nothing easy now, all blood and bruise,
mouth twisted into a wound
from where the dark words ooze.

An old train whistles past.
A finger flares on a string.
You trawl your heart's tracks for a last line,
crawl through a burning ring.

The Ballad of Síle na Gig

I
Come gather round boys and come gather round men,
I'll show ye a sight that ye won't see again,
though you may think it's little, its impact is big,
come list to my story, I'm Síle na Gig.

II
And what is a gig, did I hear you enquire?
The answer's the apex of all your desire:
a gig is the elegant carriage you see,
right under my belly: my Síle na Gee.

III
Like the gig with two wheels it can give you a ride,
you'll be cosy and cosseted snugly inside,
as a whirligig jiggles you down a green lane,
so your Síle na Gig jolts you nearly in twain.

IV
You'll be hard from Ardcath to the Tower at Rattoo,
to Kilsarkan where I have a womb with a view,
to Cashel and Doon, where I lie on my side,
holding open my casket with evident pride.

V
On to Ballynahinch where I'm clicking my heels,
come click with me, darlin', and see how it feels,
it starts like a waltz and it ends like a jig,
the dance that you'll dance with a Síle na Gig.

VI

Some say I remind them that death hurries near,
ye came into the world by the gap ye see here,
and ye'll die a wee death every time ye go in,
but there's life in me still, I'm a decent oul' skin.

VII

Some think I'm a warning put up by a bishop,
to show Adam's race what the devil can dish up.
Like Eve with her apple, I don't give a fig,
I'm a whore to the core, is old Síle na Gig.

VIII

You may hunt high and low for a maidenly kiss,
but to all who come hunting I'll promise them this,
for my womanly treasure they won't have to dig,
it's all out in the open with Síle na Gig.

IX

Call me witch, call me bitch, I'm the true divine hag,
I'm stone but not flagstone for I never flag.
A flasher, a smasher, come pimp or come prig,
I've got it, I flaunt it, says Síle na Gig.

Leonardo's Cradle Song

It seemed to me that, while I was in my cradle, a kite came to me
and opened my mouth with its tail, and struck me several times
with its tail inside my lips. (Da Vinci, Notebooks, 1504)

In my cradle I dreamed that a bird touched my lip
and my cradle rose up like a great flying ship.
Feathers shall raise us, as feathers raise birds,
though quills be our feathers, though wings
    be but words.

In my cradle I dreamed that a bird touched my lip.
I will soar like the swift, like the swallow I'll dip.
Though one without wings will be carried to heaven,
he who sits down with twelve will rise up
    with eleven.

In my cradle I dreamed that a bird touched my lip
and its claws took me up in their terrible grip.
My friends I have gathered, my table I've laid,
yet truly I say that I shall be betrayed.

In my cradle I dreamed that wings opened my mouth.
With the swallows in autumn my soul will fly south.
I have fashioned the feast of the loaf without leaven
and bread without yeast will rise upwards to heaven.

In my cradle I dreamed a great beating of wings.
Though the small bird be caged, ever louder it sings.
As the grape must be pressed so it yields the
    best wine,
my crushed heart takes wings to become the divine.

Floodgates

A Chinese woman working in Wales
births her daughter in Belfast
so that little Catherine Chen
can be an Irish citizen.

Catherine's toddler brother
means her birth would incur fines
in China, where second children
are not welcome.

In Cardiff, London, Belfast, Dublin,
people shake their heads over the One Child Policy.
What kind of country, they ask,
would make such laws?

With her Irish passport,
Catherine Chen is European.
She can live in Cardiff,
London, Belfast, Dublin.

In London and Dublin,
they are talking of floodgates.
They are flooding the airwaves
with fear of Catherine Chen.

In Dublin, there is a referendum
so that little Chens don't get Irish passports
because what kind of country
has a law like that?

The Chinese woman did not know
that in Belfast, Cardiff, London, Dublin,
Chinese children, first or second,
are not welcome.

Duty Free

Before they shackle prisoners,
take photographs of those they torture,
roll their tanks over the faces of the dead,
they stop off at Shannon Duty Free.

It is their duty
to uphold justice,
equality
and liberty for all.

But there's no duty here,
just cut-price perfumes and alcohol
en route to where they've made sure
it's life that's cheap.

They've their own meaning for rendition:
It's not an innocent performance.
It's secretly bringing men to states
where torture is allowed.

It is legal for you to kill, detain or search
whoever you choose to kill, detain or search,
while those you target are illegal combatants;
those in the way, collateral damage.

All the fragrance of Arabia will not airbrush
the truth behind your euphemisms:

The Freedom Agenda for military domination,
liberation for occupation
and how many ways
can you not say torture?

Start with *stress positions,*
enhanced coercive interrogation techniques,
sleep management, waterboarding,
special methods of questioning.

All the perfumes of Arabia
cannot sweeten
the words that put
a gloss on horror.

Peppers
for Sandy

When I heard you were moving from Paterson,
I worried about the peppers on your deck.
People can take root anywhere
but what about those pale stems weighed
    with jewels?

Creamy moonstones, amethysts ripening to garnets,
teardrops of green, tiny orange earrings,
globes yellow as a child's sun,
small spheres dark as chocolate:

You fostered nations: Thai Yellow, Chinese Red;
plucked them like flowers: Summer Sweet,
    Pretty in Purple;
flourished them like Cuban cigars:
habanero, serrano, jalapeño.

In the dim kitchen they were everywhere:
fruit and vegetable, salad, spice;
warm as welcomes, sweet as sugar,
tearjerkers, mouthfire.

The Caribbean people on your block:
Dominicans, Trinidadians,
felt the sun suddenly tropical as they passed,
stopped to marvel at this sudden burst of home.

They lifted their faces to
your deck rich as a marketplace
strung with lanterns or beads,
each plant a festive tree.

Your porch steps drew their homesick feet.
They called to bargain or barter,
and gently, from tender branches,
you picked bagfuls of their memories.

When I heard you were moving from Paterson,
I had a pang for the tang of your capsicums,
I dreamed of the collective name for them:
A heatwave, an astonishment, a perplexity of peppers.

For the moment we eke out the bag of chilis
dried to slender pods of red
that you poured from a rainbow of jars.
each one can warm a tableful.

When I heard you were moving from Paterson,
I wished you well in your new home, of course,
but I hope your deck has its own weather
and warm stems bend with jewels on your porch.

Pushing the Boat Out
for Síle Yeats

You will not sit across from me again
and smile, and say, *I think we'll push the boat out.*

These last years you gave house wines a wide berth,
went straight for the Sancerre or the Chablis.
Life's too short for the cheap stuff, you said,
Why don't we push the boat out?

Life was too short indeed for you,
so we who remain
are glad you lived for the moment
before you knew how few moments were left.

Remember the room you booked us in Milan?
That four star hotel?
Sure, why would we bother with the twin room, you said,
when the suite is a snip at eighty nine euro?
We may as well push the boat out.

Few of the hotel clients –
the impeccable suits, the stiff-haired ladies –
can have enjoyed it as we did:
We were charmed by the fake Louis Quinze chairs,
our marble sitting room,
the gold taps on the bath.
It was too lovely to leave,
so we saved on dinner by eating a picnic
on the pale silk sofas.

In London you went all the way to five star,
and blagged your way to a penthouse upgrade,
pushing the boat out like an old hand.

In the end you were too weak
to fight against the tide,
but your boat was pushed out so far
it no longer bothers with the shore.

Instead it bobs far out,
in its hold a bone-dry Sancerre,
a silver ice-bucket,
a plate of exquisite cheeses.

Its cabin is furnished
in no-holds-barred style:
Egyptian cotton sheets, *eau-de-Nil* throws,
a thick bathrobe with deep-pile slippers,
here and there, perhaps, a monogram.

You are in there now
listening to Verdi on the latest hi-fi,
a silver window opening on the foam,
the colour back in your cheeks,
the sea breeze in your hair.

It's a good job you had little faith in heaven:
Your map-reading would never take you there,
and I'm not sure how St Peter would react,
if you gave him your best smile,
and asked him for an upgrade.

Six Scenes with Olives

I

Over my parents' bed, the thick cruxifix
was a *memento mori*.
Christ could slide away to reveal
a space for water, beads and a phial
of rich oil, the extreme unction.

II

In the place of the olive press, *Gethsemane*,
he was crushed, the chrism
forced out of his shrivelling skin
and falling as blood
onto the garden.

III

In the lost Carravaggio,
Christ on the Mount of Olives,
he is buckling over two sleeping forms,
while Peter, startled awake,
is Judas in *The Taking of Christ*,
looking fearfully to the future.

IV

No one is poor who has an olive tree,
the old chef tells me.
He is looking back to Palestine,
his eyes black and soft with home.
This tree is the god in our garden.
It is not food alone.
It gives us cures and candles,
leaves to feed our goats,
summer shade and winter wood.
In my country, the olives take us over,
breathe out of our skin and hair
until we are part of each other.

V

As a child,
I was sent to the chemist for a tiny bottle.
It was the myrrh of the medicine cabinet,
warmed drop by drop for ear-ache and cradle-cap,
its scent of somewhere else, warm grass and ease.

VI

Sit opposite me now and we'll anoint our tongues,
dip our bread in unctious meadowsweet
    or bitter green,
say a rosary of olive stones.

I won't ask you to stay awake
when the world presses down,
I won't chide your lidded eyes,
your sleeping form is warmth enough.

One day this rite we share
may be extreme.
Till then, my love, I'll bless
our ordinary unction.

Catherine Ann Cullen was born in Drogheda, Co Louth and lives in Kimmage, Dublin with her husband Harry Browne and daughter Stella. As a radio producer, she has made documentaries and a series about food for RTÉ Radio 1 and produced current affairs, arts and features. She has lectured at DIT and Griffith College Dublin, and works on the Writers in Schools scheme.

Catherine Ann has published two books for children, *The Magical, Mystical, Marvelous Coat* (2001) and *Thirsty Baby* (2003) with Little, Brown (US). The former won a gold award for Poetry and Folklore from the American Parents Association. She has also written stories for the RTÉ Radio 1 series *Fiction 15*, and for *Stories for Jamie* (Blackwater Press, 2002), and scripts for animation shorts including *Rowlandson Rides Again* (Moving Still, 2006). Her first collection of poetry, *A Bone in My Throat*, was published by Doghouse in 2007. Her poetry has been used by theatre companies in London and Glasgow and by Irish singer/songwriter Pearse McGloughlin, and she is a regular contributor to RTÉ Radio 1's *Sunday Miscellany*. She is a graduate of the M.Phil in Creative Writing at Trinity College Dublin, where she is studying for a PhD in Digital Arts and Humanities.

Also available from DOGHOUSE:

Every DOGHOUSE book costs €12, postage free,
to anywhere in the world (& other known planets).
Cheques, Postal Orders (or any legal method) payable
to DOGHOUSE, also PAYPAL (www.paypal.com) to
doghousepaypal@eircom.net

*"Buy a full set of DOGHOUSE books, in time they will be
collectors' items"* - Gabriel Fitzmaurice, April 12, 2005.
DOGHOUSE
P.O. Box 312
Tralee G.P.O.
Tralee
Co. Kerry
Ireland
tel + 353 6671 37547
email doghouse312@eircom.net
www.doghousebooks.ie